SECRETS OF
LIGHT

ANNA CLAYBOURNE

Marshall Cavendish
Benchmark
New York

This edition first published in 2011 in the United States of America
by MARSHALL CAVENDISH BENCHMARK
An imprint of Marshall Cavendish Corporation

Planned and produced by Discovery Books Ltd., 2 College Street, Ludlow, Shropshire, SY8 1AN www.discoverybooks.net
Managing editor: Paul Humphrey
Editor: Clare Hibbert
Designer: sprout.uk.com Limited
Illustrator: Stefan Chabluk and sprout.uk.com Limited
Picture researcher: Tom Humphrey

Photo acknowledgments: Corbis: cover cityscape (Jon Arnold/JAI), pp 5 (Henry Watkins & Yibran Aragon/Reuters), 11tl (Fred Hirschmann/Science Faction), 29tl (DLILLC); Getty Images: pp 9 (SSPL), 10 (SSPL), 15 (Gandee Vasan), 22 (James Jordan Photography); IStockphoto: cover fibre optics (Henrik Jonsson), pp 1 (The-Tor), 6 (diane39), 16 (Pillon), 17 (Julian Barkway), 25tl (Gene Chutka); NASA: pp 7br, 20; NHPA: p 23 (Photo Researchers); Science Photo Library: p 21 (Larry Landolfi); Shutterstock Images: pp 7tl (Anton Prado), 8 (fotoadrenalina), 13 (Christian Musat), 18 (Ilja Mašík), 19 (Achtin), 27 (Darko Kovacevic), 29br (Christopher Futcher); Flavio Takemoto: cover background; Wikimedia Commons: pp 4 (Honzasoukup), 25b (Hideki Kimura, Kohei Sagawa), 26 (Joseph Nicéphore Niépce).

Other Marshall Cavendish Offices:
Marshall Cavendish International (Asia) Private Limited, 1 New Industrial Road, Singapore 536196 • Marshall Cavendish International (Thailand) Co Ltd. 253 Asoke, 12th Flr, Sukhumvit 21 Road, Klongtoey Nua, Wattana, Bangkok 10110, Thailand • Marshall Cavendish (Malaysia) Sdn Bhd, Times Subang, Lot 46, Subang Hi-Tech Industrial Park, Batu Tiga, 40000 Shah Alam, Selangor Darul Ehsan, Malaysia

Marshall Cavendish is a trademark of Times Publishing Limited

The website addresses (URLs) included in this book were valid at the time of going to press. However, because of the nature of the Internet, it is possible that some addresses may have changed, or the sites may have changed or closed down since publication. While the author, packager, and the publisher regret any inconvenience this may cause to the readers, no responsibility for any such changes can be accepted by the author, packager, or publisher.

Every attempt has been made to clear copyright. Should there be any inadvertent omission, please apply to the publisher for rectification.

Library of Congress Cataloging-in-Publication Data

Claybourne, Anna.
  Secrets of light / Anna Claybourne.
    p. cm. -- (Science secrets)
  Includes bibliographical references and index.
  ISBN 978-1-60870-139-1
  1. Light--Juvenile literature. I. Title.
  QC360.C5684 2011
  535--dc22
                          2010003941

Printed in China
1 3 6 5 4 2

Contents

What Is Light?

Light is everywhere. Every morning sunlight fills the sky, and at night we switch on the electric lights in our homes. Light shines from our cell phones and TVs and from our streets and our cities.

Light for Life

Humans, plants, and animals all need light to live. Without it, we wouldn't be able to see. Even worse, we wouldn't have any food, and there would be no life on Earth.

▼ *Early morning sunlight streams through the trees in a park in central India. The Sun is our main source of natural light.*

DAY AND NIGHT

The place where you live cannot be in daylight all of the time, because Earth spins. When your part of the world is turned away from the Sun, it is nighttime. See for yourself how night and day happen.

You will need:
• a ball or globe • a sticker
• a flashlight or small lamp

1. Place the sticker on the ball to mark where you live.

2. Darken the room as much as you can. Shine the light at the ball to act as the Sun.

3. Slowly spin the ball around. Your home moves into the light (daytime), then away from the light (nighttime).

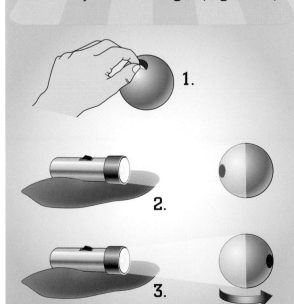

▲ Divers use flashlights to explore a flooded cave system in Mexico.

Light Energy

Light is a strange and amazing form of **energy**—like heat, electricity, and sound. What is light exactly, and where does it come from?

How far and how fast does light travel? How do our eyes see it, and how do animals and plants use it? You'll find the answers to all these questions in this book.

Where Does Light Come From?

Light is a kind of energy. Energy is the power to do work or to make things happen. There are many forms of energy, and one form can change into another.

Making Light

Light glows from objects when another kind of energy changes into light that we can see. For example, a candle contains **chemicals** that store energy. When you light it, the chemicals burn and some of the chemical energy turns into light energy.

Light Sources

Something that gives out light is called a **light source**. Candles, electric lights, and stars are all light sources. There are even some animals that produce their own light.

▼ *Even birthday candles are a light source, though they do not last for long.*

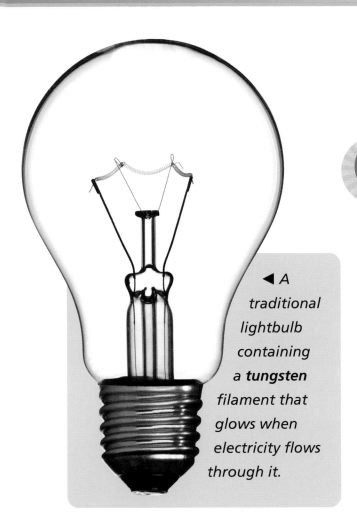

◄ *A traditional lightbulb containing a **tungsten** filament that glows when electricity flows through it.*

HOW LIGHTBULBS WORK

Lightbulbs turn electrical energy into light energy. In an old-fashioned lightbulb, electricity runs through a thin wire inside the bulb, called a **filament**. The filament heats up and glows white-hot.

In a modern energy-saving bulb, electricity flows through gases inside a glass tube, making them give out light.

▼ *A photograph of the Sun taken using a telescope, showing its churning, burning hot surface.*

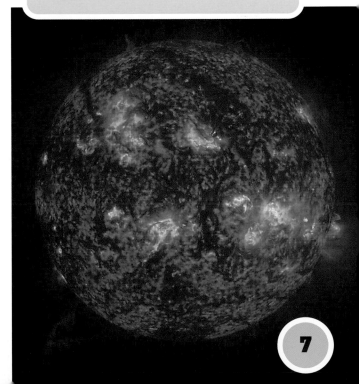

The Sun

Most of the light in our world comes from the Sun, our nearest star. It's a giant ball of gases that are constantly changing into other gases. This process gives out light and heat energy.

The Sun is so huge and powerful that it can light up the earth from 93 million miles (149 million kilometers) away. If an average lightbulb were the Sun, the earth would be the size of a pinhead, and 164 feet (50 meters) away.

What Makes a Shadow?

Light can shine through some objects, such as a glass window, but not through others. When light hits an object that it can't shine through, it makes a shadow— a dark area behind the object.

How Do Shadows Happen?

Shadows appear because light travels out from a light source in straight lines. It cannot bend around an object, so there is a dark area where the light cannot reach. The shadow is the same shape but not always the same size as the object.

Changing Shadows

Your shadow gets longer and longer as the Sun sets in the evening sky. Why is this? When the Sun is low in the sky, it shines sideways at the ground. Any object it hits, such as your body, blocks the light for a longer distance.

▼ *This camel train is blocking some of the sunlight falling on to the desert dunes, creating camel-shaped shadows.*

MAKING SHADOWS

It's easy to make a shadow much bigger than the object that casts it.

You will need:
• a flashlight, bedside light, or other small light source
• a small toy or other object

1. Make the room dark and shine your light at a plain wall.

2. Hold a small object very close to the light—try a plastic toy figure or animal. The lines, or **rays**, of light spread out from the light source, so the shadow is bigger the farther away it falls.

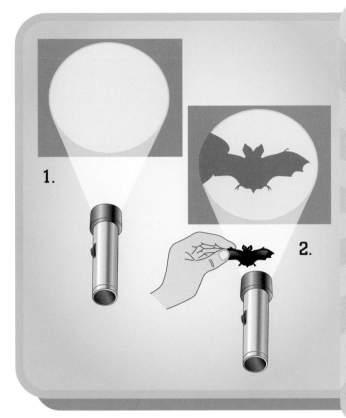

1.

2.

Shadow Clocks

The ancient Egyptians used the changing length of shadows throughout the day to make clocks. Their shadow clocks cast shadows onto a stick marked with the hours, allowing them to keep track of time.

▼ *An ancient Egyptian shadow clock. It was placed in an east-west direction and the passage of time was measured by the movement of the shadows of the twin pointers.*

What Is Light Made Of?

It is very hard to say what light is actually made of. It seems to behave in different ways depending on how you measure it, and the experiments you do.

A Wave or a Particle?

When scientists began studying light, some found that it was like a wave. A ray of light wobbles as it zooms through space, just as a wave in water wobbles the water's surface up and down. However, other scientists found that light sometimes behaves more like tiny bits of stuff, or **particles**, flying through space.

Waves and Particles

Scientists now think that both of these ideas are true. Light is a kind of wave called an electromagnetic wave. Yet it is also made up of little packages of energy, known as **photons**. Photons are like particles in some ways, but they have no **mass**—they are not made of matter. So they are not actual things. This is why they don't pile up in the corner of the room when you switch the light on!

▲ *The great scientist Isaac Newton (1643–1727) thought light must be made of particles.*

THE SPECTRUM

Light waves are part of the **electromagnetic spectrum**— a range of energy waves that includes **X rays**, **radio waves**, and **microwaves**.

All these energy waves have different **wavelengths**. Light waves have a medium wavelength and are in the middle of the electromagnetic spectrum. We call them visible light because we can see them with our eyes. Other electromagnetic waves behave just like light, but our eyes can't detect them.

▲ *The northern lights appear in the sky when tiny particles in the atmosphere give out photons, or light.*

▼ *This chart shows how waves in the electromagnetic spectrum vary from long to short. Light waves are in the middle.*

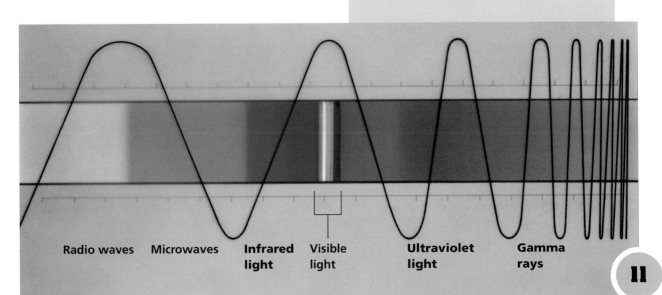

Radio waves   Microwaves   **Infrared light**   Visible light   **Ultraviolet light**   **Gamma rays**

How Do We See Light?

We live in a world full of light and have developed a great way to sense it—eyes. Seeing is incredibly useful, as it lets us use light to detect objects, find our way around, read, watch TV, and even recognize each other's faces.

Bouncing Light

As light shines from a light source, such as a lamp or the Sun, it bounces off all kinds of surfaces and objects. You can see all the things around you because of the light bouncing off objects and hitting your eyes.

▼ *This diagram shows how light from an object enters the eye. The image created on the retina is upside down, but the **brain** makes sense of it.*

SCIENCE SECRETS

INSIDE THE EYE

Your eyeball is a clever light-collecting machine. It lets light in at the front, through a hole called the **pupil**. A part called the **lens** directs the light to the back of the eyeball, where there is an area called the **retina**. It is made of light-sensing **cells** that are connected to your brain. Muscles around your eyeball can swivel and point it to look at what you want to see.

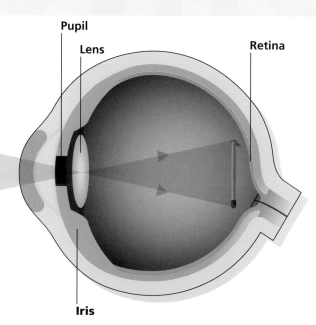

Pupil

Lens

Retina

Iris

▲ Looking at a ladybug through a magnifying glass. The lens makes the insect appear bigger.

Light Detectors

Your eyes work by collecting the light that reaches you from each object. Inside your eyes, the light hits special light sensors that send signals to your brain. Your brain also helps by making sense of the patterns your eyes see. For example, it helps you recognize things like numbers, pictures, and faces you've seen before.

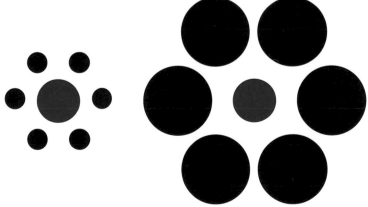

▲ Your eyes and brain can play tricks on you. In this picture, which middle circle looks bigger? In fact, they're both the same.

13

Can Light Bend?

Light travels in straight lines, but it can be made to change direction. If light hits a surface, especially a shiny surface or mirror, it can bounce or **reflect** off it, and zoom away in a new direction. If it passes through something **transparent**, it changes direction slightly, or **refracts**.

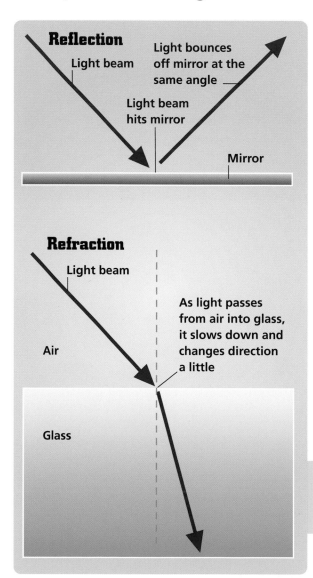

Reflection

Light beam

Light bounces off mirror at the same angle

Light beam hits mirror

Mirror

Refraction

Light beam

Air

As light passes from air into glass, it slows down and changes direction a little

Glass

Reflecting

When you look in a mirror, you see yourself. However, there aren't two of you. What you see is light from a light source that has bounced off your body, hit the mirror, and then been reflected back into your eyes.

Refracting

When light moves from one transparent substance into another, it changes direction slightly. This is why your legs look very short in a swimming pool. The light coming from your legs to your eyes changes direction as it leaves the water. It makes your legs look much shorter than they actually are.

◀ *These diagrams show light being reflected and refracted.*

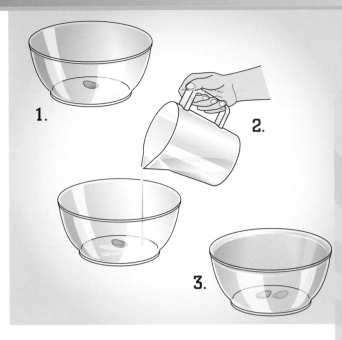

1.

2.

3.

Optical Fibers

Optical fibers are flexible tubes that can carry light along them, including around corners. The light isn't actually bending around the corners. It is just bouncing back and forth in short straight lines, reflecting off the inside wall of the fiber.

▼ *As light emerges from the end of an optical fiber, it looks like a glowing dot.*

EXPERIMENT

THE DISAPPEARING PEBBLE

This experiment appears to make a pebble mysteriously disappear.

You will need:
• a small pebble • a medium-sized glass bowl • some water

1. Put the pebble in the bottom of the bowl.

2. Fill the bowl almost to the top with water.

3. Walk around the bowl. In some positions you'll see two pebbles, and in others, the pebble will be invisible! This is because the light from the pebble changes direction as it leaves the surface and sides of the water.

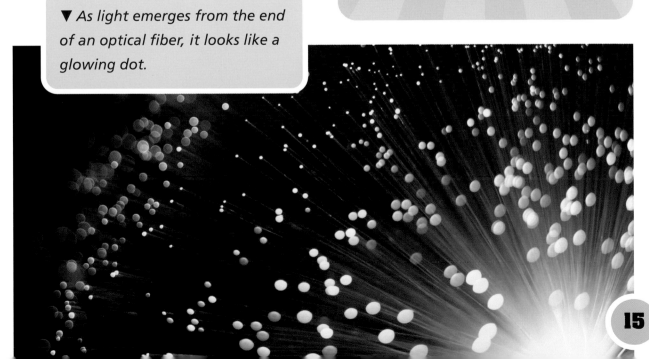

What Are Colors?

Life would be very boring without all the different colors. They are made by light waves of different lengths.

Colors of the Rainbow

The longest light waves we can see are red light. As the waves get shorter, their color moves through the rainbow, from red, orange, yellow, green, blue, indigo, and finally to violet, the shortest visible light waves.

▼ In this close-up of a TV screen, you can see the pixels (dots) of blue, red, and green light that are used to make up the picture.

Seeing Color

An object looks a particular color because its surface reflects that color of light, and so that is what our eyes sense. A carrot looks orange because it is absorbing many different colors. It reflects more orange light than any other color, so we see it as orange. We see white when all the different lengths of visible light waves are mixed together.

Animal Vision

Some animals can sense a wider range of light waves than we can. Honeybees can see ultraviolet (extra long) light waves beyond our range of vision, and some snakes can detect infrared (extra short) light waves.

▲ *When sunlight hits raindrops, it refracts and splits into a range of colors, making a rainbow.*

MAKE A RAINBOW
You can divide white light into many colors by making it shine through something transparent.

You will need:
• a clear glass jar • some water
• a piece of white paper

1. Fill a round, clear glass jar with water, and put it on a sunny window sill on a piece of white paper.

2. Where the light shines through the water and hits the paper, you should see a narrow strip of light made up of rainbow colors. The water in the jar makes the light change direction slightly, so the different wavelengths start to separate.

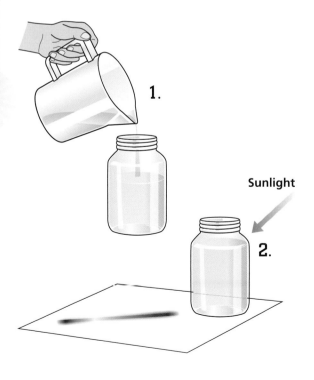

1.

Sunlight

2.

How Fast Does Light Travel?

When you switch on a light, the light seems to fill the room in an instant. In fact, light does take time to travel through space. It's just so fast that you could never follow it with your eyes.

How Fast?

The speed of light is the fastest speed that anything in the **universe** is known to travel at. It's just over 620 million miles per hour (one billion kph)—in other words, more than a million times faster than a passenger jet plane. Radio waves, X rays, and all the other waves of the electromagnetic spectrum also travel at the speed of light.

Light can slow down from this speed—for example, it travels more slowly through water than through air. However, nothing can travel as fast as light.

Crossing the Room

When you switch the light on in your bedroom, light travels across the room extremely quickly. If it is 6.5 feet (2 m) from your lamp to your wall, the light would reach the wall in approximately one 150-millionth of a second.

▼ *The fastest you are ever likely to travel is around 620 mph (1,000 kph) on a jet. Light travels a million times faster!*

SEEING STARS

When you see light from the Sun and stars, you're seeing them as they were, not as they are now. Because they are so far away, it takes a while for their light to reach us. Light from the Sun, for example, takes eight minutes to reach Earth. So the Sun actually sets eight minutes before it disappears over the horizon!

▲ *The light of the Sun reflected in these sunglasses took eight minutes to reach Earth.*

▼ *Light from the Sun travels through space and hits the half of the Earth that is facing it.*

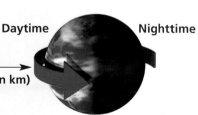

Sun

Daytime   Nighttime

← Average distance = 92.6 million miles (149 million km) →

Earth

How Far Can Light Reach?

Using your eyes, you can see a long, long way—not just down the street, or from one mountaintop to another— but billions and billions of miles out into space. You are able to see faraway planets and stars.

Light from Far Away

You don't have bionic eyes. It's just that light travels all the way from distant objects to you. When you look at the stars, you're seeing light from so far away that it has taken years to get to Earth. Some of the stars you see have actually long since gone out! Only their light is left, traveling over billions of miles to reach you on Earth.

Viewing the Past

Our most powerful telescopes, such as the Hubble Space Telescope, detect light from very distant stars and **galaxies**. These stars are so far away that the light we see from them began its journey millions or billions of years ago.

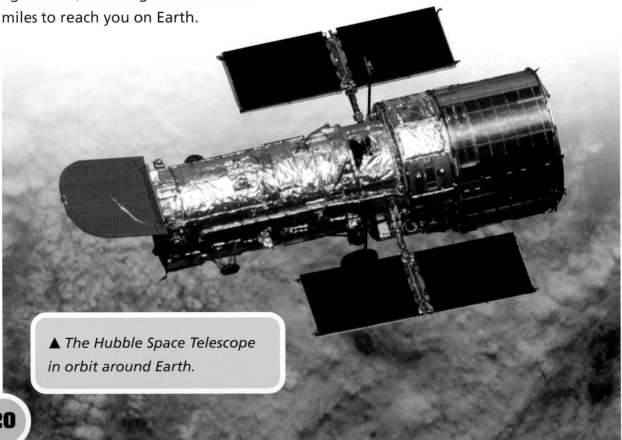

▲ *The Hubble Space Telescope in orbit around Earth.*

► *The constellation (star group) Cygnus, the Swan. The large, bright star that forms the swan's tail is Deneb, 1,600 light-years away.*

With the help of powerful telescopes, we can look back in time. We can see what was happening in the early universe, long before the earth existed.

SCIENCE SECRETS

Distances in space are often measured in **light-years**. One light-year is the distance that light travels in one year. Because light moves so fast, a light-year is a very long way— about 5.9 million million miles (9.5 million million km).

The nearest star to our own Sun is called Proxima Centauri, and it's about 4 light-years away. Others are much farther away. The star Vega is about 25 light-years away, and Betelgeuse is around 450 light-years away.

Which Animals Make Light?

Wouldn't it be weird if you had a flashing lamp on your forehead, or two rows of runway lights down your sides? Some animals do!

Living Light

Light that comes from living things is called **bioluminescence**. Some creatures light up so that they can send signals to each other. Others use lights to attract their prey. Many of the most amazing light-producing creatures live in the deepest oceans, where the Sun's light cannot reach.

Glowing Bugs

Fireflies—a type of beetle—are probably the best-known glowing animals. They flash at night with green, yellow, or reddish light to find other members of the same **species** in order to mate. In Malaysia, a type of snail also has a glowing light on its body.

▼ *A firefly with its brightly glowing tail clearly visible.*

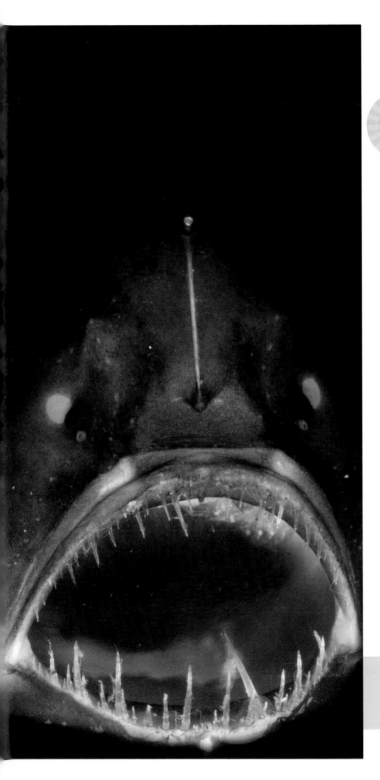

HOW ANIMALS MAKE LIGHT

Bioluminescent creatures usually make light by combining two or more chemicals inside their bodies. This causes a **chemical reaction** that gives off light.

Some animals are hosts to **bacteria** that live inside their bodies and do the glowing for them.

Deep-sea Fish

The anglerfish, a scary-looking deep-sea fish, has a glowing light dangling on a stalk on its head. When prey animals come close to investigate the light, the fish snaps them up. Some deep-sea sharks, such as lantern sharks, have patterns of lights on their bodies. Scientists think they use them to send each other signals and to help them hunt in groups.

◄ *An anglerfish lures a meal in the ocean depths.*

How Can Light Make Electricity?

We need an electricity supply in our homes, factories, shops, and schools. Electricity is made using other forms of energy —for example, by burning coal or gas in power stations.

Many of our traditional fuels are running out, and we will soon need to rely on other methods to make more of our electricity.

Electricity from the Sun

A great way to make electricity without using up fuel is to harvest light energy from the Sun. This is known as **solar power**. To turn the light into electricity, we use special substances called **photoelectric** materials. When light hits them, it makes a flow of electricity run through them.

Solar Panels

Photoelectric materials are made into large sheets called **solar panels**, which can be fixed to a rooftop or anywhere that catches the sunshine. The **electric current** they produce is carried along wires to where it is needed.

Solar panels are black because a black surface soaks up the most light, while lighter surfaces reflect more light.

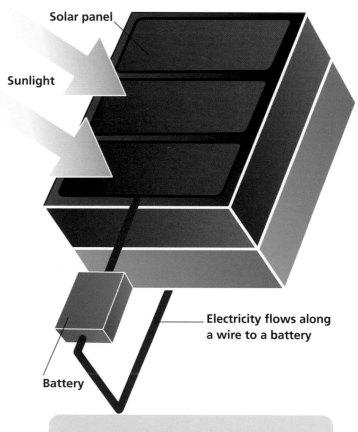

Solar panel

Sunlight

Electricity flows along a wire to a battery

Battery

▲ *A solar panel soaks up light and converts it into a flow of electricity, which can be stored in a battery.*

SOAKING UP LIGHT

Black surfaces reflect very little light—that's why they appear dark. Instead of bouncing off a black surface, light's energy enters it and turns into other energy forms, such as heat or, in a solar panel, electricity.

▲ This solar panel is being attached to someone's roof to provide their home with electricity.

▼ This race car runs on solar power. Cars like this need too many solar cells, though, to be realistic for everyday transport.

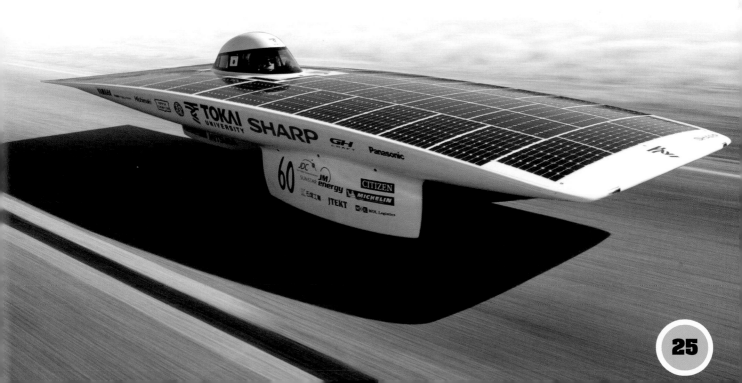

How Can Light Make Photographs?

One of the most amazing inventions that makes use of light is photography. It can capture every detail of a moment from real life, and show it as a picture on paper.

The Dark Chamber

Around one thousand years ago, Arabian scientist Alhazen made the first **camera obscura** or "dark chamber." It was a darkened room with a tiny hole in one side. This let narrow light rays from the outside shine in and make an upside-down image on the opposite wall.

▼ Joseph Niépce took the first permanent photo in 1826. It showed the view from the window of his work room.

The image was upside-down, just as the image on the back of the eye is upside-down, because light travels in a straight line. Light from objects higher than the hole travels straight down through the hole to become low in the image. Light from objects lower than the hole travels straight up through it to become high in the projected image.

Light Pictures

Artists often used a small camera obscura in a box to help them draw accurately, but they weren't able to capture the image itself.

Then, in the 1820s, French scientist Joseph Niépce was experimenting with substances that changed color when light shone on them. He coated a sheet of metal with light-sensitive chemicals and put it inside a camera obscura. Over several hours, the light patterns created a permanent image on the metal.

MAKE A CAMERA OBSCURA

The best place to try this experiment is in a room with a small window and bright sunshine outside.

You will need:
• some black cloth or paper
• some masking tape or thumbtacks • a pin

1. Cover the window completely with thick black cloth or paper. Use tape or thumbtacks to hold the covering up.

2. Make a small hole with a pin in the middle of the cloth. You should be able to see the scene outside appearing on the opposite wall, upside down.

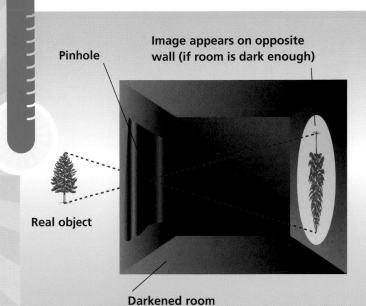

Pinhole

Image appears on opposite wall (if room is dark enough)

Real object

Darkened room

Modern Cameras

Today, cameras are more complex and can also take color pictures. Some still use light-sensitive film, but most are **digital**. Instead of light-sensing chemicals, a digital camera has **electronic** sensors that detect light and change it into electrical signals.

◀ *With a modern digital camera, you can take photos, then upload them on to your computer and print them.*

27

Why Do Living Things Need Light?

Light is essential for almost all life on Earth. Without it, there would be no plants, as they need light to grow. Most animals feed on plants, or on other animals that do. With no light, there would be no animals, including humans.

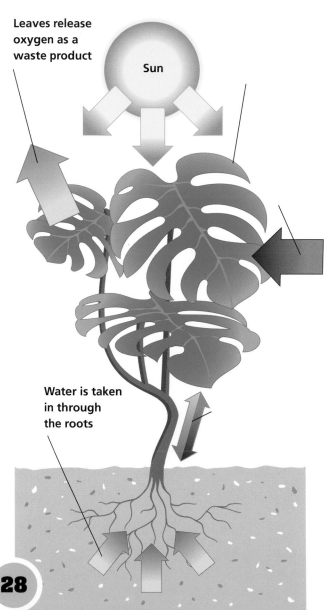

Leaves release oxygen as a waste product

Sun

Water is taken in through the roots

Photosynthesis

Plants grow by taking energy from sunlight. They turn this energy into plant matter—their leaves, stems, roots, fruits, and seeds. This process is called **photosynthesis**, which means making with light. It happens inside a plant's leaves, using a green substance called **chlorophyll** to absorb the light. That's why most plants have green leaves.

Give Me Light!

Plants can't grow without light, and they are programmed to seek it out. If you grow plants on a windowsill, they'll lean towards the glass to get as much

◄ *This diagram shows how a plant uses photosynthesis to make food from sunlight. During photosynthesis, plants take in the gas carbon dioxide and give off oxygen.*

HEALTH-GIVING LIGHT

Sunlight helps our bodies make some of the substances we need to stay healthy. One is **vitamin D**, which helps bones grow and the body fight off illnesses.

Being in the sunshine for a little while each day is good for you. However, too much strong sun can burn your skin, which is why it's important to wear sunscreen.

▲ Like all plants, bamboo makes energy from sunlight. When pandas eat bamboo, they turn the plant matter into energy to make their own bodies move and grow.

sunlight as they can. Plants will also grow around corners or even through simple mazes to get closer to the light. Seedlings shoot up from the soil towards the sunlight.

▶ All our food ultimately comes from the process of photosynthesis.

Glossary

bacterium (plural bacteria) A very tiny, simple type of living thing that has just a single cell.

bioluminescence Light given out by living things.

brain The organ at the center of the nervous system that acts like a "control room." Its jobs include processing information from the eyes and other sense organs, controlling the other organs, coordinating movement, and, in some animals, allowing activities such as memory and thought.

camera obscura A dark room or box that allows light in through a tiny hole, forming an image.

cell One of the billions of tiny living parts that make up every animal or plant. A cell is the smallest unit of life.

chemical A scientific name for a substance.

chemical reaction A process that happens when two or more chemicals combine and change.

chlorophyll A green substance in plants that helps them turn light energy into food.

digital Computerized, or working by storing information in number form.

electric current A flow of electricity.

electromagnetic spectrum A range of energy waves that includes light, X rays, and radio waves.

electronic Relating to the flow of electricity through tiny parts.

energy The ability to do work or to make changes happen.

filament A very thin wire found inside some types of lightbulb.

galaxy A huge cluster or swirl of stars in space.

gamma ray A form of electromagnetic wave with an even shorter wavelength than ultraviolet.

infrared light A form of light with a very long wavelength that is normally not visible to humans.

iris The colored part of the eye that adjusts to allow more or less light through the pupil to reach the retina.

lens A transparent, curved object used to bend and focus rays of light. Your eye has a lens that focuses light on the retina.

light source An object that light shines from.

light-year The distance that light travels in a year.

mass The amount of matter in an object. On Earth, the mass of an object is the same as its weight.

microwave A form of electromagnetic wave that has a longer wavelength than infrared light but a shorter wavelength than radio waves. Microwave ovens can be used to cook or heat food.

optical fiber A flexible glass tube that can carry light.

particle A tiny fragment or part.

photoelectric Involving the ability to convert light into a flow of electricity.

photon A tiny unit or "packet" of light energy.

photosynthesis A process that plants use to turn light energy from the Sun into plant matter.

pupil The hole in the front of the eye that lets in light.

radio wave A form of electromagnetic wave that can carry sound.

ray A beam of light.

reflect The way light bounces off a surface.

refract The way light changes direction when it passes from one transparent substance into another.

retina A patch of light-sensitive cells at the back of the eyeball.

solar panel A sheet of photoelectric material for collecting sunlight and converting it into electricity.

solar power Using energy from the Sun to provide electricity or other useful energy.

species One particular type of living thing. Members of the same species look similar and can reproduce together.

transparent Another word for see-through.

tungsten A type of metal.

ultraviolet light A form of light with a very short wavelength that is normally not visible to humans.

universe The whole of space and everything that exists.

vitamin D A chemical that people need, and can make when their bodies are exposed to sunlight.

wavelength The length from one point on a wave to the same point on the next wave.

X ray A form of electromagnetic wave that can easily pass through materials such as body tissue, so it is used by doctors for making images of the bones inside the body.

Further Information

Books
Awesome Experiments in Light and Sound by Michael A. DiSpezio (Sterling, 2006)

Extreme Science: Lights Out! by Sean Callery (A&C Black, 2009)

Fusion: Voyage of a Light Beam by Andrew Solway (Heinemann-Raintree, 2005)

Horrible Science: Frightening Light by Nick Arnold (Scholastic, 2009)

Websites
Cool Cosmos
(http://coolcosmos.ipac.caltech.edu)
Exciting interactive site all about infrared light.

Gallery of Visual Illusions
(http://faculty.washington.edu/chudler/chvision.html)
A selection of interesting optical illusions to test yourself with.

Optics for Kids
(http://www.opticalres.com/kidoptx_f.html)
Facts, diagrams, and quizzes related to the science of light.

Science Experiments for Kids: Light and Refraction
(http://www.associatedcontent.com/article/2349088/science_experiments_for_kids_light.html?cat=4)
A selection of simple light experiments to try.

Index